United States Government Accountability Office

Report to the Subcommittee on Energy and Water Development, Committee on Appropriations, U.S. Senate

June 2013

NATIONAL NUCLEAR SECURITY ADMINISTRATION

Laboratories' Indirect Cost Management Has Improved, but Additional Opportunities Exist

GAO-13-534

G A O
Accountability * Integrity * Reliability

Highlights

Highlights of GAO-13-534, a report to the Subcommittee on Energy and Water Development, Committee on Appropriations, U.S. Senate

NATIONAL NUCLEAR SECURITY ADMINISTRATION

Laboratories' Indirect Cost Management Has Improved, but Additional Opportunities Exist

Why GAO Did This Study

NNSA, a semiautonomous agency within DOE, oversees the nation's nuclear security programs. M&O contractors manage NNSA's facilities, including its national security laboratories—Lawrence Livermore, Los Alamos, and Sandia. Each year, M&O contractors spend billions of dollars to manage and operate these laboratories. Costs include both direct costs—which can be identified with a specific objective or program—and indirect costs, such as management, administrative, and facility costs. Federal Cost Accounting Standards give M&O contractors flexibility in how costs are classified as direct or indirect and allocated to programs.

GAO was asked to review M&O contractor indirect cost management. GAO examined (1) whether laboratory M&O contractors' practices differ for allocating indirect costs and, if so, how; (2) the extent to which NNSA ensures that laboratory M&O contractors' allocated indirect costs are accurate; and (3) the extent to which NNSA ensures that laboratory M&O contractors' indirect costs are reasonable. GAO reviewed NNSA and laboratory M&O contractor data and documents and spoke with DOE and NNSA officials and M&O contractors.

What GAO Recommends

GAO recommends DOE clarify the uses of the data gathered through the Institutional Cost Reporting initiative, conduct periodic risk assessments, and incorporate more specific requirements for benchmarking in its laboratory M&O contracts. DOE generally agreed with GAO's recommendations.

View GAO-13-534. For more information, contact David C. Trimble at (202) 512-3841 or trimbled@gao.gov.

What GAO Found

The National Nuclear Security Administration's (NNSA) management and operating (M&O) contractors differ in how they classify and allocate indirect costs at NNSA laboratories. Although different approaches are allowed by Cost Accounting Standards, these differences limit the ability to compare program costs across the laboratories. Recognizing the limitations of its current cost data, the Department of Energy (DOE) and NNSA are implementing the Institutional Cost Reporting initiative intended to create a standardized report of certain costs, including many indirect costs. However, DOE is uncertain how it will use the data gathered by this initiative, and these efforts may provide only limited improvements because the data will continue to only be reported at an aggregate level.

NNSA examines M&O contractors' models for allocating indirect costs for compliance with Cost Accounting Standards' requirements at least annually, which helps ensure accuracy. NNSA has identified instances when these models did not comply with these requirements, but NNSA has worked with M&O contractors to address these issues. NNSA generally relies on the M&O contractors' internal audits, however, to assess whether M&O contractors' day-to-day cost allocation practices conform to disclosed cost allocation models. NNSA reviews some summary data to independently assess day-to-day compliance with Cost Accounting Standards but does not conduct independent audits. DOE's Office of Inspector General (OIG) has audit authority at NNSA laboratories. OIG officials stated that the frequency and scope for conducting audits to assess contractors' compliance with Cost Accounting Standards should be based on the level of risk. However, NNSA and OIG officials and M&O contractors hold varying opinions regarding the level of risk that inaccurate indirect cost allocation practices at the laboratories pose. In the absence of formal, periodic risk assessments, NNSA may not have a well-documented basis for its decisions regarding the type, timing, and extent of future monitoring or oversight.

NNSA reviews M&O contractors' cost data and other information to assess the reasonableness of their costs, including indirect costs. NNSA also uses other means to help ensure the reasonableness of these costs. For example, NNSA's contracts require M&O contractors to regularly benchmark their costs to other contractors and industry. These requirements, however, do not specify the areas that should be examined, how frequently benchmarking should occur, and what process should be used for implementing any needed corrective actions. As a result, M&O contractor efforts to benchmark costs varied across laboratories.

Contents

Abbreviations

CAPE	Cost Assessment and Program Evaluation
DOD	Department of Defense
DOE	Department of Energy
M&O	Management and Operating
NNSA	National Nuclear Security Administration
OFFM	Office of Field Financial Management
OIG	Office of Inspector General

GAO

441 G St. N.W.
Washington, DC 20548

U.S. GOVERNMENT ACCOUNTABILITY OFFICE

June 28, 2013

The Honorable Dianne Feinstein
Chairman
The Honorable Lamar Alexander
Ranking Member
Subcommittee on Energy and Water Development
Committee on Appropriations
United States Senate

The National Nuclear Security Administration (NNSA)—a semiautonomous agency within the Department of Energy (DOE)—manages the nation's nuclear security programs.[1] The primary missions of these programs are to maintain the safety, security, and effectiveness of the U.S. nuclear weapons stockpile; reduce the global threat posed by nuclear proliferation and terrorism; and provide nuclear propulsion systems for the U.S. Navy. NNSA undertakes these responsibilities through eight sites. Three of these sites—Lawrence Livermore National Laboratory, Los Alamos National Laboratory, and Sandia National Laboratories—are national security laboratories. These three laboratories are critical to carrying out NNSA's mission to provide management and security of the nation's nuclear weapons programs. The laboratories also support additional missions, including nuclear nonproliferation activities and work for other federal agencies such as the Departments of Defense and Homeland Security. In fiscal year 2012, NNSA's annual appropriation was $11 billion, $4.64 billion of which funded these three laboratories.

To manage and operate its laboratories, NNSA relies on management and operating contractors, known as M&O contractors, and reimburses them for the costs incurred in carrying out NNSA's missions. These M&O contractor costs include both direct costs—costs that can be directly identified with specific cost objectives such as a program or project—and indirect costs—costs of activities that cannot be specifically identified with a specific cost objective but which indirectly support a program, such as management, administrative, and facility costs. M&O contractors are required to follow federal requirements governing NNSA indirect cost management. These include Cost Accounting Standards, which contain

---

[1]Congress created NNSA as a semiautonomous agency within the Department of Energy in 1999 (Title 32 of the National Defense Authorization Act for Fiscal Year 2000, Pub. L. No. 106-65, § 3201 et seq.).

　　　　GAO-13-534 Indirect Costs at NNSA Laboratories

requirements for the measurement, assignment, and allocation of costs to government contracts and provide criteria for the classification and allocation of indirect costs. These standards also provide contractors with some flexibility in how they classify and allocate indirect costs.[2] In addition, the Federal Acquisition Regulation requires that these costs be reasonable, among other things. In recent years, according to NNSA officials, indirect costs have accounted for about half of these three laboratories' budgets.

We have reported on NNSA's indirect costs in the past. In 2005, we reported that indirect costs at NNSA's laboratories could not be readily compared because of differences in how indirect costs are identified and allocated to programs, and because of differences in the facilities' missions, corporate structures, and accounting systems.[3] In 2010, we reported that NNSA does not collect reliable and timely information on indirect costs at the NNSA sites, including the laboratories, which is crucial for effective management of government operations and for oversight.[4] In 2012, we identified opportunities for the laboratories to streamline their support functions, which include many indirect costs.[5] Further, NNSA's and the DOE Office of Environmental Management's contract and project management for major projects—$750 million or greater—remain on our list of programs at high risk of fraud, waste, abuse, and mismanagement or are in most need of transformation.[6] In addition to our concerns, the Department of Defense (DOD), which depends on NNSA to assess and maintain the reliability and safety of the nuclear weapons stockpile and helps fund these efforts, has expressed concerns about NNSA's ability to accurately understand and assess its major program costs. The National Defense Authorization Act for 2013,[7]

---

[2]See appendix II for description of Cost Accounting Standards applicable to laboratory M&O contractors.

[3]GAO, *Department of Energy: Additional Opportunities Exist for Reducing Laboratory Contractors' Support Costs*, GAO-05-897 (Washington, D.C.: Sept. 9, 2005).

[4]GAO, *Nuclear Weapons: Actions Needed to Identify Total Costs of Weapons Complex Infrastructure and Research and Production Capabilities*, GAO-10-582 (Washington, D.C.: June 21, 2010).

[5]GAO, *Department of Energy: Additional Opportunities Exist to Streamline Support Functions at NNSA and Office of Science Sites*, GAO-12-255 (Washington, D.C.: Jan. 31, 2012).

[6]GAO, *High-Risk Series: An Update*, GAO-13-283 (Washington, D.C.: Feb. 14, 2013).

[7]Pub. L. No. 112-239, 126 Stat. 1632 (2013).

as well as the Nuclear Weapons Council,[8] tasked the Office of the Secretary of Defense's Cost Assessment and Program Evaluation (CAPE) to work with NNSA to develop more accurate cost estimates for its weapons programs.

You asked us to review M&O contractor indirect cost management at NNSA's national security laboratories. Our report examines: (1) whether laboratory M&O contractors' practices differ for allocating indirect costs and if so, how; (2) the extent to which NNSA ensures that laboratory M&O contractors' allocated indirect costs are accurate; and (3) the extent to which NNSA ensures that laboratory M&O contractors' indirect costs are reasonable.

To determine whether laboratory M&O contractors' practices differ for allocating indirect costs, and if so, how, we reviewed federal Cost Accounting Standards, which in part guide M&O contractor allocation practices, and NNSA and M&O contractor documentation associated with complying with these standards. We met with officials from NNSA's Office of Field Financial Management (OFFM) in Albuquerque, New Mexico. We also visited Lawrence Livermore, Los Alamos, and Sandia national laboratories and interviewed NNSA field office officials and M&O contractors. We reviewed NNSA and contractor documents showing the actions taken by NNSA and the M&O contractors to manage indirect costs at the three laboratories, as well as data on these costs. We reviewed indirect cost data used by M&O contractors to document compliance with Cost Accounting Standards and manage indirect costs and met with knowledgeable NNSA officials and M&O contractors to assess the reliability of these data. We found them to be sufficiently reliable for the purposes of this report. To gather additional perspectives on how differences in cost allocation practices affect stakeholders, we met with officials from DOD's CAPE to discuss their review of the laboratories' costs and possible ways to improve the data collected that is needed to support cost analysis informed decision making across the NNSA laboratories and sites.

To examine the extent to which NNSA ensures that laboratory M&O contractors' reported indirect costs are accurate, we reviewed reports prepared by each contractor's internal audit function. We also interviewed

---

[8]The Nuclear Weapons Council coordinates activities jointly managed by DOD and DOE to support the nuclear stockpile.

NNSA officials and M&O contractors to discuss steps taken to ensure compliance with federal Cost Accounting Standards and interviewed officials from the DOE Office of Inspector General (OIG) to determine their role in assessing M&O contractors' compliance.

To examine the extent to which NNSA ensures that laboratory M&O contractors' indirect costs are reasonable, we reviewed pertinent documents and interviewed NNSA officials and M&O contractors about steps taken to assess the reasonableness of indirect costs. We also reviewed the M&O contracts in place in fiscal year 2012 and fiscal year 2012 performance evaluations of the laboratory M&O contractors to identify the financial incentives, if any, provided to M&O contractors to manage costs, including indirect costs. We reviewed studies completed during the period from 2008 to 2012 to assess the reasonableness of laboratories' costs. Additional details on our objectives, scope, and methodology can be found in appendix I.

We conducted this performance audit from April 2012 to June 2013 in accordance with generally accepted government auditing standards. Those standards require that we plan and perform the audit to obtain sufficient, appropriate evidence to provide a reasonable basis for our findings and conclusions based on our audit objectives. We believe that the evidence obtained provides a reasonable basis for our findings and conclusions based on our audit objectives.

Background

M&O contractors operate and maintain NNSA's three national security laboratories, as well as the infrastructure necessary to support the nuclear weapons stockpile and the capabilities to conduct the scientific, technical, engineering, and production activities that ensure the continued safety and reliability of the stockpile. These laboratories perform various forms of weapons research and development activities as follows:

- Los Alamos National Laboratory in Los Alamos, New Mexico, operated by Los Alamos National Security, LLC,[9] is responsible for nuclear components and providing unique capabilities such as neutron scattering and radiography. Los Alamos also manufactures plutonium components and weapons detonators.

---

[9]Los Alamos National Security, LLC, is an organization managed by the University of California; Bechtel National, Inc.; The Babcock & Wilcox Company; and URS Corporation.

- Lawrence Livermore National Laboratory in Livermore, California, operated by Lawrence Livermore National Security, LLC,[10] is responsible for nuclear components and providing unique capabilities in high-energy density physics; high explosives research, development, and assessment; and environmental containment of high-hazard experiments.

- Sandia National Laboratories in Albuquerque, New Mexico, and Livermore, California, operated by Lockheed Martin Corporation, is primarily responsible for nonnuclear components, including environmental testing of nuclear weapons systems, nonnuclear component engineering, and some nonnuclear component production.

NNSA and DOE officials are responsible for a variety of oversight functions at the laboratories. For example, NNSA oversees and conducts annual performance reviews of its M&O contractors at each laboratory. OFFM, which includes the field Chief Financial Officer, is primarily responsible for ensuring the integrity of the laboratories' financial management systems, including the proper allocation of direct and indirect costs. In addition, NNSA maintains an on-site presence at each of the laboratories through field offices that assist in the daily management of the M&O contractor. The DOE OIG, which has audit authority at NNSA laboratories, assists NNSA in carrying out its oversight responsibilities by conducting independent audits as necessary.[11]

In general, federal contractors such as NNSA's M&O contractors are subject to federal Cost Accounting Standards. These standards provide direction for the consistent and equitable distribution of contractors' costs to help federal agencies more accurately determine the actual costs of its contracts. Table 1 briefly describes Cost Accounting Standards. Appendix II describes these standards in more detail.

---

[10]Lawrence Livermore National Security, LLC, is an organization managed by Bechtel National, University of California, Babcock and Wilcox, Washington Division of URS Corporation, and Battelle.

[11]NNSA relies on the combined efforts of the DOE OIG, OFFM, M&O contractor internal audit management, and others, as outlined in the Cooperative Audit Strategy published in 1992, as well as other audit and assessment processes, to monitor indirect and direct costs on an ongoing basis.

Table 1: Cost Accounting Standards

Cost accounting standard	Brief description
401	Requires consistency in estimating, accumulating, and reporting costs
402	Requires consistency in allocating cost incurred for the same purpose
403	Addresses allocation of home office expenses
404	Addresses capitalization of tangible assets
405	Addresses accounting for unallowable costs
406	Addresses cost accounting period
407	Addresses use of standard costs for direct material and direct labor
408	Addresses accounting for costs of compensated personal absences
409	Addresses depreciation of tangible capital assets
410	Addresses allocation of business unit general and administrative expense to cost objectives
411	Addresses accounting for acquisition costs of material
412	Addresses composition and measurement of pension costs
413	Addresses adjustment and allocation of pension costs
414	Addresses cost of money as an element of the cost of facilities capital
415	Addresses accounting for the cost of deferred compensation
416	Addresses accounting for insurance costs
417	Addresses cost of money as an element of the cost of capital assets under construction
418	Addresses allocation of direct and indirect costs
420	Addresses accounting for independent research and development costs and bid and proposal costs

Sources: GAO analysis based on information provided by NNSA officials and general Cost Accounting Standards information.

Note: Cost Accounting Standard 419 was consolidated with Cost Accounting Standard 418 and therefore no longer exists.

In addition to Cost Accounting Standards, M&O contractors, DOE, and NNSA must comply with other federal requirements, including the Federal Acquisition Regulation and DOE financial management and accounting orders. In particular, the Federal Acquisition Regulation applies to federal agencies to help regulate the policies and procedures for acquisitions for the government. A requirement of this regulation is that a contractor's costs must be reasonable.

We previously reported that indirect costs could not be readily compared across laboratories and discussed steps DOE has taken to try to provide more comparability of its costs.[12] Specifically, in 2005, we reported that differences in how indirect costs are identified and allocated to programs and differences in the facilities' missions, corporate structures, and accounting systems affected the comparability of costs across laboratories.[13] In that report, we noted that while DOE required its M&O contractors to separately report data on costs to support missions, such as administrative support, these costs could not be readily compared. These include costs that are classified as both direct and indirect. Further, in 2012, in response to limitations in these data, we reported that DOE was trying to improve its ability to oversee its M&O contractors' costs through the implementation of the Institutional Cost Reporting initiative.[14] Specifically, this initiative is a multiyear effort that aims to collect certain cost data and report them at an aggregate level across broad cost categories such as maintenance and central administrative support.

M&O Contractors Differ in How They Allocate Indirect Costs, and Efforts to Standardize Cost Reporting May Provide Limited Improvements

M&O contractors differ in how they classify and allocate indirect costs, which continues to make it difficult for NNSA, Congress, and others to compare program costs across laboratories. Recognizing the limitations of its cost data, DOE and NNSA are implementing the Institutional Cost Reporting initiative, but this initiative may only provide limited improvements over existing data.

---

[12]GAO-05-897 and GAO-12-255.

[13]GAO-05-897.

[14]GAO-12-255.

Differences in How M&O Contractors Allocate Indirect Costs Limit the Comparability of Program Costs across Laboratories

M&O contractors' differ in how they allocate indirect costs to specific programs, as allowed by Cost Accounting Standards. To allocate costs to programs, M&O contractors classify costs as either direct or indirect. Direct costs, such as labor and materials, are assigned to the benefitting program or programs. Indirect costs—those costs that cannot be assigned to a particular program such as costs for administration and site support—are accumulated, or grouped, into indirect costs pools. The M&O contractor estimates the amount of indirect costs (accumulated into indirect cost pools) that will need to be distributed to each program and adjusts the costs to actual costs by the end of the fiscal year. The contractor then distributes these costs based on a rate in accordance with the cost allocation model. Typically, labor costs receive a higher allocation of indirect costs than do costs such as direct material expenditures. The final program cost is the sum of the total direct costs plus the indirect costs distributed to the program (see fig. 1).

Figure 1: Overview of Management and Operating (M&O) Contractor Process for Identifying Costs as Direct or Indirect and Allocating to Programs

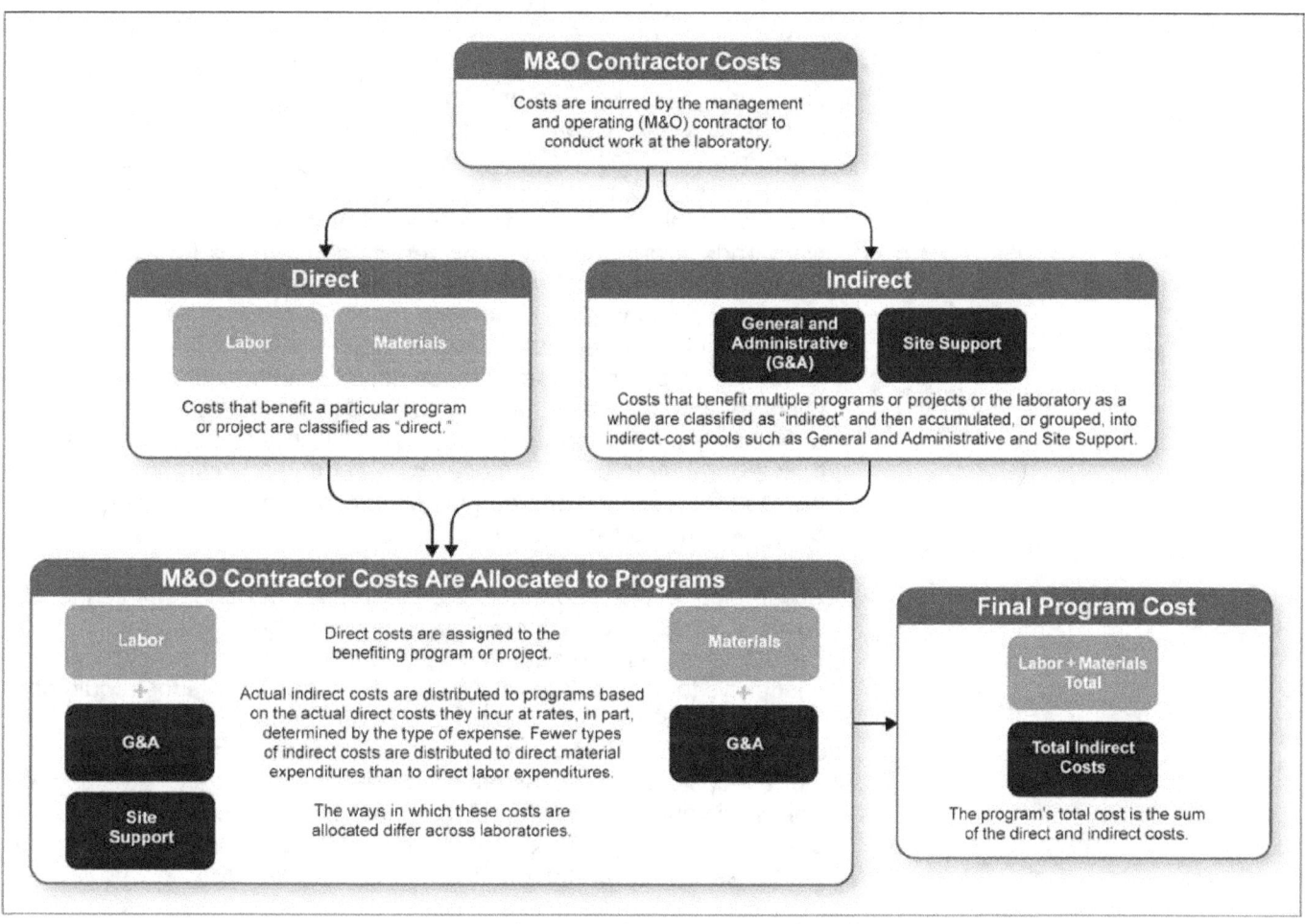

Sources: GAO analysis of NNSA and M&O contractor documentation.

Note: We use the term programs in this report to mean efforts managed by M&O contractors.

In implementing this allocation process, however, similar costs can be allocated differently because M&O contractors' cost allocation models, which outline the M&O contractor's structure for identifying and allocating indirect costs, differ. Officials in NNSA's OFFM said that because of the flexibility the Cost Accounting Standards provide, NNSA does not have the authority to require M&O contractors to classify and allocate costs in a uniform manner. Specifically, M&O contractor cost allocation models differ in how they (1) classify costs as either direct or indirect, (2) accumulate these costs into indirect cost pools, and (3) distribute indirect costs to specific programs. For example:

- *Classification.* M&O contractors differ in how they classify costs as direct or indirect. For example, M&O contractors at Los Alamos told us they make significant use of service centers—departments which perform specific technical or administrative services for programs such as for telecommunications and computing and separately assign these costs directly to the benefitting laboratory department overheads or programs. In total, service center costs for fiscal year 2012 totaled around $180 million at Los Alamos. In contrast, M&O contractors at Lawrence Livermore reported making limited use of service centers—their costs totaling around $20 million for fiscal year 2012—and instead classified these costs as indirect. Lawrence Livermore officials said that they conducted a business process analysis, which found that it was more efficient and cost-effective for their laboratory to allocate these costs through an indirect-cost pool than to try to develop and administer service centers that would then charge each program directly.

- *Accumulation.* M&O contractors differ in how they accumulate indirect costs into indirect-cost pools. For example, the M&O contractor at Sandia used both program management and division support indirect-cost pools to accumulate certain indirect support costs that could not be charged to specific projects. The M&O contractors at Los Alamos and Lawrence Livermore recovered these costs through different indirect-cost pools such as program office overhead and site support. For fiscal year 2011, we found that M&O contractors accumulated costs into differing numbers of indirect-cost pools, with one site using as few as 4 pools and another using as many as 11.

- *Distribution.* M&O contractors differ in how they distribute indirect costs accumulated into indirect-cost pools to programs. For example, in fiscal year 2013, the M&O contractor at Lawrence Livermore distributed General and Administrative costs—costs incurred for the administration of the lab such as executive management and human resources—to total costs excluding materials and subcontract costs incurred by programs, while the M&O contractor at Los Alamos distributed these costs to total program costs including those for labor, materials, and subcontract costs.

M&O contractors' cost allocation models have also substantially changed over time. For example, according to M&O contractor documentation for Los Alamos, the M&O contractor substantially changed and simplified its cost allocation model in fiscal year 2013 to improve compliance with Cost Accounting Standards and increase the transparency of these costs. M&O contractor documentation outlining the major changes indicated that these changes increased administrative efficiency at the laboratory. While the change in the cost allocation model did not change the total amount of indirect costs allocated at the laboratory, the changes did affect the amount of indirect costs allocated to certain program costs, such as the cost of subcontractors employed at the laboratory and construction projects, which now received a greater distribution of indirect costs. The M&O contractor at Lawrence Livermore also substantially changed its cost allocation model in recent years. For example, for fiscal years 2005 to 2013, the M&O contractor decreased the number of different rates used to allocate indirect costs to its programs from 184 to 12. The M&O contractor at Sandia has also substantially changed its cost allocation model since fiscal year 2010. For example, the M&O contractor combined certain indirect pools and changed the amount of indirect costs allocated to some program costs, such as those for subcontractor labor.

Because of the differences in how M&O contractors allocate indirect costs and changes in allocation practices over time, it remains difficult to compare program costs either across laboratories or at an individual laboratory over time. In particular, it is unclear whether the allocation differences or other factors, such as more effective program management, were the primary cause for the difference in program costs. Specifically, differences in how costs are classified as either indirect or direct, accumulated into indirect-cost pools, and distributed to specific programs can impact the ratio of indirect to total program costs at the laboratories. This ratio is, in part, used by Congress to compare M&O contractor performance. However, as we have previously reported, this ratio alone should not be used as a tool to compare performance as it does not account for the myriad factors that can affect the ratio of indirect to total program costs.[15] Specifically, data on these costs do not account for differences in M&O contractor allocation practices or differences in laboratories' mission, size, age, or condition, which affects costs. For example, the maintenance costs for a 50-year-old manufacturing facility will likely be higher than those of a modern research facility.

---

[15]GAO-05-897.

DOE officials noted that Cost Accounting Standards do not require all contractors to use the same methodology to allocate indirect costs and that project management and cost estimation can be conducted through a variety of project management tools. However, GAO has previously noted shortcomings with data collected, as well as its use by DOE and NNSA to manage projects and estimate costs. For example, in 2010, we reported that NNSA cannot accurately identify the total costs to operate and maintain weapons facilities and infrastructure. In 2011, we reported that NNSA needs more comprehensive infrastructure and workforce data to improve its enterprisewide decision making. Further, in 2012, we reported that NNSA lacked the analytical capability needed to review proposals for program activities and verify cost estimates. Additionally, according to a senior CAPE official responsible for working with NNSA to develop more accurate cost estimates for its weapons programs, the cost data collected by NNSA's M&O contractors has shortcomings. According to the official, M&O contractors organize their cost data to meet two primary goals. First, contractors want to ensure that they are fully reimbursed for their costs. Second, contractors want to ensure that they fairly allocate indirect costs to programs and projects. However, the CAPE official stated that these data are of limited use to support decision making for programs, projects, and activities including weapons life extension programs, facility construction projects, and facility operations. The official stated that, during his team's review, they found that the M&O contractors' cost data for the laboratories was rarely in a form that would be useful for decision-making analysis. In addition, the official stated that the quality of data varied widely across M&O contractors and substantial effort by the CAPE team and the M&O contractor was required to understand and explain trends in the data. The CAPE official added that NNSA does not currently have the data needed to accurately identify the total costs to operate and maintain its weapons facilities and structures. The official stated that NNSA's needs are changing rapidly as officials deal with difficult choices in a budget-constrained environment. He added that the need for better cost data collection to support decision making is both immediate and imperative. The official stated that CAPE is actively working with NNSA to guide and improve its ability to gather, analyze, and present more useful M&O contractor cost data to decision makers. In May 2013, NNSA announced the creation of the Office of Program Review and Analysis, to provide independent analytical advice to help improve NNSA's ability to budget, plan, and oversee programs.

DOE and NNSA Are Taking Additional Steps to Standardize the Reporting of Certain Indirect Costs, but These Efforts May Provide Only Limited Improvements

DOE and NNSA are taking steps to standardize the reporting of certain costs; however, these efforts may provide only limited improvements because the data will continue to only be reported at an aggregate level. As noted previously, in 2010, DOE began implementation of Institutional Cost Reporting—a DOE-wide initiative to create a standardized report of certain costs, including many indirect costs—to improve its ability to oversee its sites' costs. Specifically, Institutional Cost Reporting is a system to collect and report costs at an aggregate level across 28 broad cost categories. DOE officials and documentation noted several anticipated improvements that are expected from implementing Institutional Cost Reporting, including improved data reliability as compared with previous method for collecting and reporting support costs. In January 2012, we recommended that DOE take steps to ensure that the data resulting from the Institutional Cost Reporting are complete and comparable for monitoring sites' support costs, and DOE concurred with our recommendation.[16] DOE established joint DOE and contractor teams to perform peer reviews intended in part to standardize the data collected through Institutional Cost Reporting. In May 2013, DOE officials said that they had completed the reviews for several sites, including Lawrence Livermore, Los Alamos, and Sandia. Officials stated that they were uncertain when the remaining reviews would be completed.

According to DOE documents, the Institutional Cost Reporting initiative established general goals to develop more timely, accurate, and meaningful data on M&O contractor's costs. However, DOE officials responsible for helping implement the initiative stated that they are uncertain how or if the data will actually be used. This is because this initiative replaced an earlier system used by DOE to collect and report support costs and, like this earlier system, the Institutional Cost Reporting data will only provide data at an aggregate level across cost categories, such as maintenance. In addition, DOE officials told us that since the Institutional Cost Reporting data appear at an aggregate level, further analyses will be needed to assess the causes for any differences in Institutional Cost Reporting cost categories across the laboratories and other sites. For example, if costs for an activity such as maintenance are significantly higher at one laboratory than another, further research would be needed to determine if the difference is due to efficiency or differences in mission, condition of infrastructure, location, or other reasons. A senior DOE official said that Institutional Cost Reporting is in its early stages and

---

[16]GAO-12-255.

that DOE does not currently know how the data will be used. Further, DOE officials said they were uncertain about the extent to which Institutional Cost Reporting data can be used to improve the transparency and management of laboratory costs, especially indirect costs. To better understand the Institutional Cost Reporting data and help identify potential management uses, DOE officials said that they had initiated several analyses to review specific cost items in the Institutional Cost Reporting data. However, a DOE official helping oversee these efforts noted that the data gathered through Institutional Cost Reporting may ultimately not prove to be useful, as it may not provide meaningful data that can be used to aid management and oversight. Officials with DOD's CAPE office have also expressed concerns over the usefulness of these aggregated data to improve transparency, aid management, and identify opportunities for cost savings. Moreover, in commenting on a draft of this report, DOE noted that it has determined that the Institutional Cost Reporting initiative data are aggregated at such a high level that they cannot be used to compare detailed contractor costs.

OFFM officials also stated that their use of the Institutional Cost Reporting data to assess costs and potentially identify cost savings is still largely in the planning stages. Specifically, OFFM officials stated that, while the Institutional Cost Reporting data is more useful and comparable than other data, such as indirect cost rates, additional analyses are still needed to determine if the cost differences identified in Institutional Cost Reporting data are due to efficiency differences or other differences among the laboratories. To date, OFFM officials have taken some steps to use Institutional Cost Reporting data to compare costs across its laboratories and help identify cost savings. For example, NNSA officials said they used Institutional Cost Reporting data to help compare M&O contractor costs. Following this comparison, OFFM is now planning an effort to reduce the amount of state taxes paid by its M&O contractors.

NNSA Takes Some Steps to Assess the Accuracy of M&O Contractors' Indirect Cost Allocations

NNSA has taken steps to examine the accuracy of M&O contractors' cost allocation models, but actions to independently assess day-to-day cost allocation practices have been more limited. Specifically, NNSA's OFFM examines laboratory M&O contractors' cost allocation models for compliance with Cost Accounting Standards requirements, which helps ensure accuracy. NNSA generally relies on M&O contractors' internal audits to assess whether day-to-day cost allocation practices conform to disclosed M&O contractor models. NNSA's efforts to independently assess M&O contractors' day-to-day cost allocation practices to ensure compliance with Cost Accounting Standards are more limited.

NNSA Examines Laboratory M&O Contractors' Cost Allocation Models for Compliance with Cost Accounting Standards

NNSA's OFFM examines laboratory M&O contractors' detailed cost allocation models for compliance with Cost Accounting Standards each time a contractor changes its model, which typically occurs upon initiation of the contract and at least annually thereafter. Specifically, within 60 days before a contractor implements changes in a new cost allocation model, the contractor must submit the proposed changes—in a document called a disclosure statement—to OFFM for a compliance review. These disclosure statements include a summary and justification of proposed changes, a reference to the Cost Accounting Standards that apply to each change, and information on the anticipated impact of the proposed changes on a program area's costs. OFFM reviews the disclosure statement to determine whether the proposed change is adequately described and complies with applicable Cost Accounting Standards. In doing so, OFFM typically follows a detailed review plan or checklist adapted as necessary for the review, including conducting on-site visits or follow-up with the contractor to ensure the disclosed changes to the model are in compliance with Cost Accounting Standards. Based on this review, OFFM sends its recommendation for approval of the disclosure statement to the contracting officer, who then makes the determination to approve.

OFFM works with laboratory M&O contractors to try to bring cost allocation models into compliance with Cost Accounting Standards and has identified instances when a laboratory's cost allocation model did not comply with Cost Accounting Standards. Some of these instances affected the accurate allocation of indirect costs. OFFM officials stated that instances of noncompliance have been resolved or are in the process of being resolved. Examples are as follows:

- In March 2009, OFFM and NNSA site officials determined that the M&O contractor's indirect cost allocation model for Lawrence Livermore did not fully comply with Cost Accounting Standards. Specifically, activities such as science and technology strategic planning and laboratory outreach were included in a strategic mission support indirect-cost pool. These costs were viewed by Lawrence Livermore as broadly institutional in the same manner as General and Administrative costs. According to NNSA officials, the M&O contractor allowed this practice to occur because it believed that these programs did not equitably benefit from the activities covered by these indirect costs. OFFM officials disagreed, and the M&O contractor changed its cost allocation model in fiscal year 2013 to include these indirect costs in the General and Administrative indirect-cost pool.

- In October 2009, OFFM reviewed M&O contractor indirect cost allocations at Lawrence Livermore being applied to the National Ignition Facility—a research facility intended to demonstrate nuclear fusion reactions using lasers—and determined that the M&O contractor's cost allocation model did not comply with certain aspects of the Cost Accounting Standards. Specifically, the M&O contractor's model did not equitably distribute indirect costs during the construction of the facility, as the Cost Accounting Standards require. NNSA's contracting officer concurred but permitted the M&O contractor to continue using this model through October 2012 to minimize disruption to the program. As a result, 18 other programs at the site continued to assume a greater share of these indirect costs, which totaled about $134 million for fiscal year 2013, according to our analysis of M&O contractor documents. For example, according to M&O contractor documents, the Departments of Defense and Homeland Security, which conduct research at Lawrence Livermore, paid more each year to cover indirect costs that would have otherwise been collected from the National Ignition Facility project.

- In July 2010 and January 2011, OFFM determined that the M&O contractor's indirect cost allocation model for Los Alamos did not fully comply with Cost Accounting Standards because construction projects and certain other types of labor were fully or partially exempt from having to contribute the standard cost allocation amounts for General and Administrative indirect costs at the laboratory. According to OFFM officials, other programs at the site needed to contribute more money to the General and Administrative cost pool to compensate for this shortfall, resulting in the inequitable sharing of these indirect costs across all programs. Los Alamos changed its allocation model in fiscal year 2013 to eliminate these exemptions and more equitably share these indirect costs across all programs.

NNSA Generally Relies on M&O Contractors' Internal Audits to Assess Whether Day-to-day Cost Allocation Practices Conform to Disclosed M&O Contractor Models

Officials with NNSA's OFFM told us that they generally rely on the M&O contractors' internal audit efforts to assess whether M&O contractors' day-to-day cost allocation practices conform to their disclosed cost allocation models. OFFM officials told us that they perform some limited testing to verify that M&O contractors' practices conform to their cost allocation models but that they largely rely on the M&O contractors' internal audit groups to perform this verification.[17] M&O contractors' internal audits have found that some contractor allocation practices do not conform to their models. Internal audits at all three of the laboratories identified some problems—particularly with how labor hours are charged to projects, but NNSA officials stated that these problems are not significant in relation to the costs incurred by M&O contractors. According to OFFM officials, M&O contractors, and documents, the laboratories have corrected or are in the process of correcting these problems, and follow-up audits are also being conducted at some sites to verify that problems are adequately addressed. Following are examples:

- *Los Alamos.* In 2009, Los Alamos' M&O contractor conducted an internal audit to determine whether its laboratory's day-to-day labor allocation practices conformed to its disclosed cost allocation model. The audit determined that labor hours reported by M&O contractor employees did not always reflect the actual work performed, and labor costs may not have been allocated equitably among all benefitting programs and therefore was not consistent with their cost allocation model. For example, one employee interviewed during the contractor's internal audit noted an instance where labor hours were transferred from one program to another to prevent a cost overrun. The M&O contractor identified and implemented corrective actions to address the problem, including providing training and guidance to laboratory employees about proper time and labor reporting practices. In April 2011, the M&O contractor's internal audit office conducted a follow-up audit and found that three of four corrective actions identified in the prior report were completed but that there was still need for further improvement regarding the allocation of labor costs. Specifically, the follow-up report concluded that the allocation of indirect labor costs posed a high risk and significant concern. According to the M&O contractor documentation, M&O contractor managers later determined that the problem was not significant

---

[17]These internal audits are conducted by the M&O contractors' internal audit group or at times performed by external audit firms under contract with the M&O contractor.

enough to warrant further corrective action. However, the M&O contractor's internal audit management and OFFM officials told us that they are continuing to work to resolve the issue.

- *Lawrence Livermore.* Lawrence Livermore's M&O contractor internal auditors reported similar problems in September 2010, including some instances where indirect labor hours were inaccurately allocated to direct projects, inconsistent with its disclosed cost allocation model. To correct these problems, M&O contractor managers agreed to update policies, procedures, and guidance on proper cost allocation practices at the laboratory, and develop training for employees. The M&O contractor's internal audit office plan for fiscal year 2013 states that it expects to review the results of prior internal audits to determine the need for additional audits in specific areas.

- *Sandia.* Based on the problems found at the other two laboratories, an NNSA Sandia Field Office official recently asked its M&O contractor's internal audit office at Sandia to verify Sandia's labor hour allocations. Sandia's internal audit office reported in October 2012 that M&O contractor employees were not always accurately allocating their time in accordance with actual work performed. Corrective actions in response to this audit are still being implemented. Specifically, the M&O contractor agreed to improve guidance and training provided to all employees about proper time charging practices and policies, and to conduct periodic self-assessments to ensure compliance with these practices and policies.

NNSA's Efforts to Independently Assess M&O Contractors' Day-to-day Cost Allocation Practices for Compliance With Cost Accounting Standards Are Limited

Although NNSA's OFFM has responsibility for supporting contracting officers in the day-to-day oversight of M&O contractors' management of indirect costs, its role does not include conducting independent audits to assess compliance with Cost Accounting Standards, according to OFFM officials. On a limited basis, however, OFFM reviews some summary M&O contractor data to determine whether actual cost allocation practices are consistent with disclosed practices and complies with applicable federal requirements, and conducts expanded reviews, as needed. Specifically, M&O contractors must annually submit a formal statement documenting the total size of their indirect-cost pools and allocations, as well as the indirect rates used during the previous fiscal year. In addition to these steps, OFFM can request audit assistance from the OIG—which has audit authority at NNSA laboratories.

OIG officials stated that the frequency and scope for conducting audits for contractors' compliance with Cost Accounting Standards should be based on the level of risk. However, OFFM and OIG officials and M&O contractors hold varying opinions regarding the level of risk of inaccurate indirect cost allocation practices at the laboratories. For example, some OFFM and OIG officials and M&O contractors told us that they believe the risk is generally low compared with other federal agencies. Specifically, because NNSA M&O contractor operations are federally funded, and the operations are not mixed with private activities, the risk is low that federal funds are being used to pay an inequitable and higher share of indirect costs for private, nonfederal activities. In contrast, senior NNSA field office official told us that he is concerned about the ongoing possibility that indirect costs could be manipulated—that is, allocated to other programs—to avoid exceeding program budgets and, therefore, believes the risk is high. This concern was echoed by an M&O contractor's internal audit office, which reported in April 2011 that, based on its audit findings the allocation of indirect costs posed a high risk. This contractor's internal audit office also confirmed that M&O contractor labor hours in at least one instance were transferred to another program to prevent a cost overrun. Despite the uncertainty of the risk of noncompliance, NNSA's Chief Financial Officer in OFFM does not conduct formal periodic risk assessments. One of the federal standards for internal control—risk assessment—states that management should assess the risks faced entity-wide,[18] and at the activity level, from both external and internal sources. The standard also states that if risks have been identified, management should decide what actions should be taken to mitigate them. The identification and prioritization of these risks can then influence decisions regarding the type, timing, and extent of future monitoring or oversight. Risk identification methods may include, among other things, forecasting and strategic planning, and consideration of findings from audits and other assessments. Without a formal, periodic risk assessment regarding the level of risk posed by noncompliance, NNSA may not have a well-documented basis for its decisions regarding the type, timing, and extent of future monitoring or oversight.

Recently, the OIG has taken some steps to improve its understanding of the risks associated with M&O contractors' noncompliance with Cost Accounting Standards. First, the OIG contracted a private auditing firm to perform a limited audit at Lawrence Livermore in 2012 to test compliance with one Cost Accounting Standard that addresses the allocation of direct

---

[18]*GAO, Standards for Internal Control in the Federal Government,* GAO/AIMD-00-21.3.1 (Washington, D.C.: November 1999).

and indirect costs.[19] In April 2013, the OIG reported that no compliance problems or potential issues or challenges were identified. Second, in January 2013, OIG officials stated that they were developing additional guidance to ensure that field staff document their consideration of these risks in their annual assessments, as necessary.

NNSA Reviews M&O Contractor Information and Uses Other Means to Help Ensure the Reasonableness of Indirect Costs

NNSA reviews M&O contractor information to assess the reasonableness of M&O contractor costs, including indirect costs, at the laboratories. NNSA also uses other means to help ensure the reasonableness of costs, such as requiring M&O contractors to compare costs with other laboratories and industry, but these efforts vary across laboratories.

NNSA Reviews M&O Contractor Information to Assess Whether Indirect Costs Are Reasonable

NNSA reviews M&O contractor information and cost data to assess the reasonableness of M&O contractor costs at the laboratories. In order for a contractor's costs to be reimbursed, they must be reasonable. The Federal Acquisition Regulation provides that a cost is reasonable based on a number of considerations and circumstances, including whether the type of cost is generally recognized as ordinary and necessary for the conduct of the contractor's business or the contract performance.[20] To demonstrate compliance with the Federal Acquisition Regulation, M&O contractors submit summary and some detailed information and data on their costs to NNSA and the OIG for review and approval. For example, according to DOE guidance, M&O contractors are required to annually prepare and submit summary information identifying costs incurred during the year. This information is then reviewed by NNSA's field office Chief Financial Officer, contracting officers located at the laboratories, and the OIG, among others. Further, NNSA contracting officers told us that they

---

[19]The OIG also contracted with an audit firm to perform audits of compliance with Cost Accounting Standards at the Savannah River Site. An audit report is still in the process of being developed.

[20]Federal Acquisition Regulation, 48 C.F.R. § 31.201-3.

review the M&O contractors' own system of internal controls for ensuring that incurred indirect costs comply with contract provisions, such as by reviewing the M&O contractors' internal audits assessing the reasonableness of their costs. Contracting officers serve a principal role in ensuring the reasonableness of M&O contractor costs, as required in the Federal Acquisition Regulation. Decisions to approve M&O contractor costs are documented in contracting officers' approval memos, however, the specific steps taken in these reviews to determine reasonableness are not documented. In addition to the contracting officers' review efforts, OFFM officials stated that they review M&O contractors' high-level summary indirect cost information to help ensure the reasonableness of M&O contractor costs. OFFM officials stated that they act in a supporting role to the review efforts of the contracting officers in helping to ensure the reasonableness of M&O contractors' costs.

NNSA Uses Other Means to Help Ensure the Reasonableness of Costs, but These Efforts Vary Across Laboratories

NNSA also uses other means to encourage M&O contractors to manage the laboratories in a cost-efficient and effective manner. In particular, NNSA includes provisions in its contracts to encourage or require laboratories to take steps to manage costs. For example, NNSA's contracts require M&O contractors to regularly benchmark costs to standards for high performing external businesses and other contractors. Laboratory M&O contractors take some steps to benchmark costs and practices to industry and take corrective actions as needed, but these efforts have varied from laboratory to laboratory. For example, the M&O contractor at one laboratory stated that they undertook a benchmarking study to compare the costs of servicing the laboratory's fleet of vehicles in-house as compared with using an outside vendor. The M&O contractor, concluding that an outside provider would be more cost-effective, contracted with an outside provider and estimated an annual savings of approximately $775,000. In addition to M&O contractor-led efforts, NNSA has also taken steps to benchmark costs at its laboratories and sites. Specifically, NNSA hired external consulting groups to conduct benchmarking studies in the areas of finance, information technology, and human resources management across multiple NNSA sites, which provided their reports to NNSA in March 2009.[21] These studies identified areas for improvement and, while M&O contractors noted that they consider the information from these studies in decision-making processes, they were unable to provide documentation showing what steps were taken specifically in response to findings or recommendations in these studies.

Although contracts for the three laboratories do require that benchmarking be performed, the contract provisions do not specify the areas that should be examined, how frequently benchmarking should occur, and what process should be used for implementing any needed corrective actions. In contrast, DOE provides more specific requirements for benchmarking pension and post-retirement benefit costs.[22] Specifically, DOE guidance requires contractors to benchmark certain employee benefits every 2 to 3 years and implement corrective action plans if benchmarking efforts show that the value of certain employee benefits are 5 percent or higher than industry averages.

In addition to benchmarking, OFFM is involved in other activities to help identify cost savings, improve efficiency, and help ensure the reasonableness of costs. We previously reported on efforts taken by DOE and NNSA to reduce M&O contractors' costs at its laboratories such as through streamlining and centralizing certain support functions, such as for human resources.[23] In addition to those efforts, the OIG also conducts audits to help reduce costs, including indirect costs. OFFM officials said that they also participate in NNSA's Business Management Advisory Council, which includes NNSA's Chief Operating Officer, chief operating officers from each M&O contractor, field office representatives, and the NNSA Senior Procurement Executive. The Business Management Advisory Council meets quarterly to discuss proposals and initiatives to improve efficiency and identify cost savings. For example, we previously

---

[21]Hackett Group, *Achieving World Class Performance: Finance and HR Benchmark Results Executive Briefing,* March 2009. Grant Thornton, *Department of Energy National Nuclear Security Administration Enterprise Optimization Consulting Services Initial Assessment,* March 16, 2009. Aon Consulting, *National Nuclear Security Administration Acquisition Strategy Team (AST); Part I: Analysis of Retirement Income Benefit Issues by Acquisition Option,* and *Part II: Analysis of Health Care Benefit Issues by Acquisition Option,* March 19, 2009.

[22]DOE Order 350.1, Chg 3, Contractor Human Resource Management Programs

[23]GAO-12-255.

reported that, in 2011, the Business Management Advisory Council considered consolidating human resource and other services at all of NNSA's sites to achieve cost savings.[24]

To further encourage M&O contractors to manage the laboratories in an effective and efficient manner, NNSA also includes performance-based fees in its contracts. Specifically, field office contracting officials rate the M&O contractors' efforts to identify and implement cost-savings measures, while also achieving mission goals, through annual performance evaluation plans. These cost management efforts also include efforts to identify and implement cost-savings measures. However, according to NNSA officials, the amount of performance-based fee tied to cost management efforts is relatively small—$1 million or less at each laboratory annually—and may not provide a meaningful incentive to the contractors. In contrast, the overall incentive fees for laboratory M&O contractor work can be up to $60 million annually. NNSA officials stated that, because financial incentive amounts are limited, mission work could be negatively impacted if financial incentives were redirected to improving cost management at the laboratories.

NNSA is exploring ways to improve the use of incentives in its contracts to encourage M&O contractors to manage the laboratories in an efficient and effective manner. Specifically, according to NNSA officials, NNSA added requirements in the proposed combined contract for its Y-12 and Pantex sites in fiscal year 2013, which would link future contract extensions to cost-savings goals to improve cost management.[25] For example, these new provisions would have required the M&O contractors to achieve at least 80 percent of the proposed cost-savings measures, as outlined in their contractual language, in order to receive a contract extension. However, we have questioned these anticipated cost savings because of the limited details available about the actual work that will be consolidated, and the adequacy of data used to estimate cost savings.[26]

---

[24]GAO-12-255.

[25]The Y-12 National Security Complex in Oak Ridge, Tennessee, manufactures components for nuclear weapons, including uranium components, evaluates, tests, assembles, and disassembles these components; supplies highly enriched uranium for use in naval reactors. The Pantex Plant in Amarillo, Texas, evaluates, repairs, and dismantles nuclear weapons; conducts high explosive research and development.

[26]GAO, Modernizing The Nuclear Security Enterprise: The National Nuclear Security Administration's Proposed Acquisition Strategy Needs Further Clarification and Assessment, GAO-11-848 (Washington, D.C.: Sept. 20, 2012).

As of June 2013, the status of NNSA's combined contract award for the Y-12 and Pantex sites is uncertain. On April 29, 2013, we sustained portions of bid protests regarding this combined contract. Specifically, we concluded that NNSA failed to meaningfully assess the majority of each offeror's proposed cost savings, and based its source selection decision on the unsupported assumption that all cost savings proposed by every offeror would be achieved. The protest decision recommended that NNSA reopen the procurement for this contract and request additional information from the offerors about their proposed cost savings.[27] Following this decision, in May 2013, NNSA announced that it would reopen competition for the combined contract. Because the contract has not yet been implemented, it is too soon to evaluate the effectiveness of these new contract provisions, but NNSA officials stated they anticipate incorporating similar provisions into future contracts for the laboratories.

Conclusions

It is critical that NNSA and its M&O contractors ensure that the billions of dollars spent each year at the laboratories are used effectively. Because Cost Accounting Standards allow flexibility in how M&O contractors classify and allocate direct and indirect costs to programs, however, it can be difficult to assess cost data and meaningfully compare cost management performance across laboratories. Recognizing these challenges, DOE has been developing the Institutional Cost Reporting initiative to separately collect data on certain costs, including many indirect costs, in an effort to improve its ability to oversee M&O contractors' costs, including, indirect costs, at the NNSA laboratories. The initiative is still under development, however, and the uses for the data collected have not been determined. Without a clearer understanding of how Institutional Cost Reporting data can be used to manage costs and what data are needed, it is unclear if this initiative will provide meaningful improvement over existing data.

NNSA has made progress in improving M&O contractors' cost allocation models to better comply with Cost Accounting Standards. However, key officials hold differing views about the level of risk of inaccurate indirect cost allocation practices at the laboratories. OIG officials stated that the frequency and scope for conducting audits for contractors' compliance

---

[27]Nuclear Production Partners, LLC, and Integrated Nuclear Production Solutions, LLC., B-407948, April 29, 2013.

with Cost Accounting Standards should be based on the level of risk. However, OFFM does not conduct periodic, formal risk assessments of contractor compliance to determine the level of risk. Without such assessments, NNSA does not have important information needed to make decisions about the type, timing, and extent of future monitoring or oversight.

In addition to efforts to assess the accuracy of indirect costs, NNSA and M&O contractors also use benchmarking as a means to assess the reasonableness of costs. Although DOE orders and M&O contracts define specific benchmarking requirements for pension costs, contracts are less specific in terms of what types of indirect costs should be benchmarked, how frequently benchmarking should take place, and the process for ensuring corrective actions are taken, as needed. Without more consistent and comparable benchmarking, NNSA will likely lack useful data about costs across the laboratories, as well as in the private sector, that could inform cost management decisions at the laboratories and identify areas for cost savings.

Recommendations for Executive Action

To help improve its ability to oversee M&O contractor costs, including indirect costs, for its laboratories and make more effective use of DOE and contractor resources, we recommend the Secretary of Energy take— or, as appropriate, direct the Administrator of NNSA to take—the following three actions:

- Clarify how data collected by the Institutional Cost Reporting initiative will be used.

- Direct OFFM to conduct formal, periodic risk assessments of M&O contractors' compliance with Cost Accounting Standards by using (1) laboratory M&O contractor internal audit results, (2) OIG audit results, and (3) other relevant information obtained through ongoing monitoring and oversight to provide a well-documented basis for its future monitoring and oversight, including determining the appropriate level of OIG audit assistance needed.

- Incorporate more specific benchmarking requirements into future laboratory contracts—similar to the benchmarking requirements used by DOE to assess and manage pension and post-retirement benefit costs—including which costs should be benchmarked, how frequently benchmarking should occur, and what process should be used to ensure corrective actions are taken, as needed.

We provided a draft of this report to DOE for its review and comment. In written comments, NNSA's Associate Administrator for Management and Budget, responding on behalf of DOE and NNSA, wrote that DOE agreed with our report's three recommendations. DOE's written comments on our draft report are included in appendix III. DOE also provided technical comments, which we incorporated into the report as appropriate.

In response to our first recommendation that DOE clarify how data collected by the Institutional Cost Reporting initiative will be used, DOE stated in its written comments that it will clarify the uses of the data, and that its estimated completion for this action is September 30, 2013. However, DOE stated that it has determined that the data are aggregated at such a high level that they cannot be used to compare detailed contractor costs. We remain concerned that, without better cost data, DOE and NNSA may continue to be limited in their abilities to effectively oversee M&O contractor costs. DOE agreed with our second recommendation that it conduct formal, periodic risk assessments of M&O compliance with Cost Accounting Standards. In its comments, DOE stated that OFFM will conduct such assessments and that its estimated completion date for this action is September 30, 2013. The agency also agreed in principle to our third recommendation that it incorporate more specific benchmarking requirements into future laboratory contracts, similar to its benchmarking requirements used to assess and manage pension and postretirement benefit costs, stating that it would evaluate options to determine appropriate benchmarking requirements for inclusion in future M&O contracts. DOE stated that the estimated completion for this action is December 31, 2013.

DOE also provided a general comment referencing our draft report's discussion of the flexibility afforded NNSA's eight integrated contractors by Cost Accounting Standards and the cost data collected by NNSA. In particular, DOE stated that the Cost Accounting Standards intentionally afford flexibility for all government contractors and that our report leaves the false impression that NNSA is somehow required to create consistency, when current practices are intentionally designed for flexibility. As stated in our report, we agree that Cost Accounting Standards provide flexibility for contractors and provided additional clarification in the report. DOE stated that the repeated statements about "flexibility" and how the current data do not address CAPE-identified requirements are misleading to the average reader who may not distinguish between the appropriateness of accounting practices and the separate issue of collecting data from accounting and other project management systems. DOE noted that project management and cost estimation are done through a variety of project management tools and that, as presented, the report would give the impression that NNSA is somehow not "accounting" for costs appropriately, and it is factually incorrect to suggest that accounting practices that adhere to applicable law are somehow askew. We recognize that there are various methods to gather data, however, as our previous work and CAPE's work have noted, these data have shortcomings for supporting decision making for programs, projects, and activities. NNSA also stated that it agreed that efforts to produce information to better support decision making from existing data could be improved. We continue to believe that improved data could aid DOE and NNSA in their efforts to oversee and manage sites' costs.

We are sending copies of this report to the Secretary of Energy, the NNSA Administrator, the appropriate congressional committees, and other interested parties. In addition, the report is available at no charge on the GAO website at http://www.gao.gov.

If you or your staff members have any questions about this report, please contact me at (202) 512-3841 or trimbled@gao.gov. Contact points for our Offices of Congressional Relations and Public Affairs may be found on the last page of this report. GAO staff who made major contributions to this report are listed in appendix IV.

David C. Trimble
Director, Natural Resources and Environment

Appendix I: Objectives, Scope, and Methodology

This report examines (1) whether laboratory Management and Operating (M&O) contractors' practices differ for allocating indirect costs and, if so, how; (2) the extent to which National Nuclear Security Administration (NNSA) ensures that laboratory M&O contractors' allocated indirect costs are accurate; and (3) the extent to which NNSA ensures that laboratory M&O contractors' indirect costs are reasonable.

To determine whether laboratory M&O contractors' practices differ for allocating indirect costs, and, if so, how, we reviewed federal Cost Accounting Standards, which, in part, guide M&O contractor allocation practices, and NNSA and M&O contractor documentation associated with complying with these standards. We met with officials from NNSA's Office of Field Financial Management (OFFM) in Albuquerque, New Mexico. We also visited Lawrence Livermore, Los Alamos, and Sandia National Laboratories and interviewed M&O contractors and NNSA field office officials. We reviewed NNSA and contractor documents showing the actions taken by NNSA and the M&O contractors to manage indirect costs at the three laboratories, as well as data on these costs. We reviewed indirect cost data used by M&O contractors to document compliance with Cost Accounting Standards and manage indirect costs and met with knowledgeable NNSA officials and M&O contractors to assess the reliability of these data. We found them to be sufficiently reliable for the purposes of this report. To gather additional perspectives on how differences in cost allocation practices affect stakeholders, we met with the Office of the Secretary of Defense's Cost Assessment and Program Evaluation (CAPE) office to discuss their review of the laboratories' cost accounting systems to improve cost estimation for weapons stockpile programs. To describe DOE and NNSA's Institutional Cost Reporting initiative, we spoke with DOE officials in its headquarters and Germantown, Maryland, offices for financial management and accounting and NNSA officials in OFFM. We also reviewed DOE and NNSA internal guidance, as well as documents describing this initiative.

To examine the extent to which NNSA ensures that laboratory M&O contractors' reported indirect costs are accurate, we reviewed relevant federal requirements, in particular, federal Cost Accounting Standards. We also interviewed OFFM officials and M&O contractors to discuss whether and how these standards apply to laboratory M&O contractors and the steps taken to ensure that M&O contractor cost allocation models comply with applicable standards. In addition, we obtained specific information regarding OFFM's identification of key instances where the M&O contractors' cost allocation models did not comply with these standards, how they did not comply, and the general status of actions to correct any significant problems. To determine the extent to which NNSA ensures that laboratory M&O contractor's day-to-day cost allocation practices conform to their disclosed cost allocation models, we interviewed OFFM, M&O contractor internal audit, and DOE Office of Inspector General (OIG) officials. As appropriate, we reviewed relevant past audits at each of the laboratories, the associated corrective actions taken and planned, and general plans for future audits. To understand the OIG's historical involvement in conducting independent audits of Cost Accounting Standards at NNSA laboratories, we reviewed relevant correspondence between NNSA and the OIG, and met with OIG officials to clarify their role in conducting past and future audits.

To examine the extent to which NNSA ensures that laboratory M&O contractors' indirect costs are reasonable, we reviewed pertinent documents and interviewed NNSA officials and M&O contractors about steps taken to assess the reasonableness of indirect costs. We reviewed requirements relating ensuring the reasonableness of costs, including the Federal Acquisition Regulation, DOE's accounting handbook, and DOE orders. We reviewed the M&O laboratory contracts in place in fiscal year 2012 to identify requirements for managing costs, including indirect costs. We also identified any requirements in the contracts for benchmarking efforts and financial incentives, if any, to encourage cost management. We reviewed performance evaluations of the laboratory M&O contractors to identify any information related to the reasonableness of costs or the effectiveness of cost-savings initiatives. We also reviewed pertinent NNSA and contractor documents related to the review and approval of M&O contractor costs, including reasonableness. We reviewed pertinent studies performed by NNSA, M&O contractors, or outside consulting firms that were completed between 2008 and 2013 related to assessing or addressing the reasonableness of laboratories' costs. We reviewed NNSA requirements linking M&O contract extensions to cost-savings initiatives to help ensure the reasonableness of costs, including the proposed combined contract for the Y-12 and Pantex sites. We met with officials from OFFM in Albuquerque and also visited Lawrence Livermore, Los Alamos, and Sandia National Laboratories to interview M&O contractors and NNSA field office officials on their efforts to ensure cost reasonableness at the laboratories, and to discuss any opportunities for improvement in this area.

We conducted this performance audit from April 2012 to June 2013 in accordance with generally accepted government auditing standards. Those standards require that we plan and perform the audit to obtain sufficient, appropriate evidence to provide a reasonable basis for our findings and conclusions based on our audit objectives. We believe that the evidence obtained provides a reasonable basis for our findings and conclusions based on our audit objectives.

GAO-13-534 Indirect Costs at NNSA Laboratories

Appendix II: Federal Cost Accounting Standards

Cost Accounting Standard	Description
401: Consistency in Estimating, Accumulating, and Reporting Costs	The cost accounting practices used in accumulating and reporting of actual cost must be consistent with the practices used in estimating costs in pricing proposals. The purpose of the standard is to enhance the likelihood that comparable transactions are treated alike and to obtain improved reliability of estimates and comparisons with performance.
402: Consistency in Allocating Cost Incurred for the Same Purpose	The same type of cost must be consistently classified as direct or indirect with respect to all work performed. The purpose of this standard is to require that each type of cost is allocated only once and on only one basis to any contract or other cost objective in order to prevent overcharging of some contracts and to eliminate double counting.
403: Allocation of Home Office Expenses to Segments	Establishes the criteria for allocation of home office expenses to segments and minimizes the amount of such expenses classified as residual.
404: Capitalization of Tangble Assets	Facilitates the consistent measurement of costs based on a capitalization policy that adheres to the criteria of the standard.
405: Accounting for Unallowable Costs	The purpose of this standard is to facilitate the negotiation, audit, and settlement of unallowable costs.
406: Cost Accounting Period	Provides criteria for the periods to be used as cost accounting periods for contract estimating, accumulating, and reporting of cost.
407: Use of Standard Costs for Direct Material and Direct Labor	Provides criteria for using standard costs for estimating, accumulating, and reporting costs of direct material and direct labor. The standard also provides criteria regarding the establishment of standards, accumulation of standard costs, and disposition of variances from standard costs.
408: Accounting for Costs of Compensated Personal Absences	Provides criterion for assigning these compensated personal costs to the cost accounting period in which the related entitlement is earned.
409: Depreciation of Tangble Capital Assets	Provides criteria for assigning costs of tangible assets to cost accounting periods and for consistent allocation of those costs to cost objectives.
410: Allocation of Business Unit General and Administrative Expense to Cost Objectives	Provides criteria for the allocation of the cost of general and administrative expenses based on their beneficial or causal relationships.
411: Accounting for Acquisition Costs of Material	This standard requires the contractor to have written statements of accounting policies and practices for accumulating the costs of material and for allocating costs of material to cost objectives.

Cost Accounting Standard	Description
412: Composition and Measurement of Pension Costs	Establishes the components of pension costs and the bases for measuring such costs. It also provides criteria for determining the amount of pension costs to be assigned to cost accounting periods.
413: Adjustment and Allocation of Pension Costs	Provides for adjustment of pension cost for actuarial gains and losses, their assignment to cost accounting periods, and bases for allocation of pension costs to business segments.
414: Cost of Money as an Element of the Cost of Facilities Capital	Provides for the explicit recognition of the cost of money for facilities capital as an element of contract costs.
415: Accounting for the Cost of Deferred Compensation	Provides criteria for the measurement and assignment of deferred compensation costs to cost accounting periods. The cost of deferred compensation is to be assigned to the cost accounting period in which the contractor incurs an obligation to compensate the employee.
416: Accounting for Insurance Costs	Provides criteria for the measurement of insurance costs, the assignment of such costs to cost accounting periods, and their allocation to cost objectives.
417: Cost of Money as an Element of the Cost of Capital Assets Under Construction	Establishes criteria for the measurement of the cost of money attributable to capital assets under construction, fabrication, or development as an element of the cost of those assets.
418: Allocation of Direct and Indirect Costs	Provides for consistent determination of direct and indirect costs, provides criteria for the accumulation of indirect costs, including service center and overhead costs in indirect-cost pools, and provides guidance relating to the selection of allocation measures based on the beneficial or causal relationship between an indirect-cost pool and cost objectives.
420: Accounting for Independent Research and Development Costs and Bid and Proposal Costs	Provides criteria for the accumulation of independent research and development costs and bid and proposal costs. It also provides criteria for the allocation of such costs to cost objectives based on the beneficial or causal relationship between such costs and cost objectives.

Sources: GAO analysis based on information provided by NNSA and the Department of Defense.

Note: Cost Accounting Standard 419 was consolidated with Cost Accounting Standard 418 and therefore no longer exists.

Appendix III: Comments from the National Nuclear Security Administration

Department of Energy
National Nuclear Security Administration
Washington, DC 20585

June 18, 2013

Mr. David Trimble
Director
Natural Resources and Environment
Government Accountability Office
Washington, DC 20458

Dear Mr. Trimble:

Thank you for the opportunity to review the Government Accountability Office's (GAO) draft report titled "*NATIONAL NUCLEAR SECURITY ADMINSTRATION: Laboratories' Indirect Cost Management Has Improved but Additional Opportunities Exist, GAO-13-534.*" I understand the GAO began this review in response to a request made by the Subcommittee on Energy and Water Development, Senate Committee on Appropriations, and was asked to examine: (1) whether laboratory Management and Operating (M&O) contractors' practices differ for allocating indirect costs and, if so, how; (2) the extent to which the National Nuclear Security Administration (NNSA) ensures that the laboratory M&O contactors' allocated indirect costs are accurate; and (3) the extent to which NNSA ensures that laboratory M&O contractors' indirect costs are reasonable. Based on their findings, the GAO provided three recommendations for executive action, focusing on clarifying planned usages for indirect cost data collected, formalizing risk assessment, and providing more specificity in contractor benchmarking requirements.

NNSA agrees with the recommendations, and the enclosure to this letter provides our detailed response which identifies the milestones and timelines for addressing the GAO's findings. In addition, we have provided general and technical comments to enhance the clarity and factual accuracy of the report. If you have any questions regarding this response, please contact Dean Childs, Director, Office of Audit Coordination and Internal Affairs, at (301) 903-1341.

Sincerely,

Cynthia A. Lersten
Associate Administrator
For Management and Budget

Enclosure

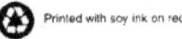
Printed with soy ink on recycled paper

Response to GAO Draft Report, GAO-13-534
"NATIONAL NUCLEAR SECURITY ADMINSTRATION: Laboratories' Indirect Cost
Management Has Improved but Additional Opportunities Exist"

The Government Accountability Office (GAO) recommended the Secretary of Energy take - or, as
appropriate, direct the Administrator of the National Nuclear Security Administration (NNSA) to
take - the following actions:

Recommendation 1: Clarify how data collected by the Institutional Cost Reporting initiative
will be used.

Management Response: Concur

The Department of Energy (DOE) Office of Chief Financial Officer will clarify the use of the
Institutional Cost Report (ICR) which provides aggregated integrated contractor cost data in
certain categories. After completing several integrated contractor peer reviews of the ICR report,
we determined that the data are aggregated at such a high level that the report cannot be used to
compare detailed contractor costs. The estimated completion date for this action is September
30, 2013.

Recommendation 2: Conduct formal, periodic risk assessments of Management and Operating
Contractors' (M&O) compliance with Cost Accounting Standards (CAS) by using: (1) laboratory
M&O contractor internal audit results; (2) Office of Inspector General (OIG) audit results; and
(3) other relevant information obtained through ongoing monitoring and oversight to provide a
well documented basis for its future monitoring and oversight. including determining the
appropriate level of OIG audit assistance needed.

Management Response: Concur

The NNSA Office of Field Financial Management (OFFM) will conduct formal, periodic risks
assessments of M&O compliance with CAS, which will incorporate the following elements: (1)
laboratory M&O contractor internal audit results; (2) OIG audit results; and (3) other relevant
information obtained through ongoing monitoring and oversight. OFFM will include
recommendations for OIG and internal audit assistance as part of the formal risk assessment
process. The estimated completion date for this action is September 30, 2013.

Recommendation 3: Incorporate more specific benchmarking requirements into future
laboratory contracts, similar to the benchmarking requirements used by DOE to assess and
manage pension and post retirement benefit costs. including which costs should be benchmarked,
how frequently benchmarking should occur and what process should be used to ensure corrective
action are taken as needed.

Management Response: Concur in Principle

NNSA agrees in principle with the recommendation and will evaluate options in order to
determine appropriate benchmarking requirements for inclusion in future Management and
Operating contracts to include detailing which costs should be benchmarked, how frequently

1

Response to GAO Draft Report, GAO-13-534
"NATIONAL NUCLEAR SECURITY ADMINSTRATION: Laboratories' Indirect Cost
Management Has Improved but Additional Opportunities Exist"

benchmarking should occur and what process should be used to ensure corrective action are taken as needed. The estimated completion date for this activity is December 31, 2013.

2

Response to GAO Draft Report, GAO-13-534
"NATIONAL NUCLEAR SECURITY ADMINSTRATION: Laboratories' Indirect Cost
Management Has Improved but Additional Opportunities Exist"

General Comment

GAO's report repeatedly references the flexibility afforded NNSA's eight Integrated Contractors by Cost Accounting Standards (as established by Public Law 100-679), and states that changes in allocation methodologies make it difficult to compare program costs across laboratories or at an individual laboratory over time. It may be helpful if the report noted that under the Public Law, the Cost Accounting Standard Board - chaired by the Office of Management and Budget (OMB) – sets the definitions for Cost Accounting Standards (CAS) and that the Board intentionally affords flexibility for all government contractors for a variety of reasons. As written, the report leaves the false impression that NNSA is somehow required to create consistency, when current practices are intentionally designed for flexibility.

GAO also quotes a senior official of the Cost Assessment and Program Evaluation (CAPE) organization as indicating that cost data collected by NNSA Integrated Contractors has shortcomings regarding support of decision making for programs, projects and activities including weapons life extension programs, facility construction projects, and facility operations. NNSA would recommend that the report emphasize that CAPE's assessments reflect concerns that CAPE has about the data to meet CAPE requirements. The current CAS standards are designed to meet the requirements of a variety of customers and users, not just a particular stakeholder. It is likely that other stakeholders would disagree with CAPE regarding what data are needed.

While not explicitly stated, these repeated statements about "flexibility" and how the current data does not address CAPE-identified requirements is misleading to the average reader who may not distinguish between the appropriateness of accounting practices and the separate issue of collecting data from accounting and other project management systems (for example, the Institutional Cost Reporting Initiative). Project management and cost estimation is done through a variety of project management tools - the institutional cost report does not, and should not, be driving overall NNSA project cost projections and project management. As presented, the report would give the impression that NNSA is somehow not "accounting" for costs appropriately, and it is factually incorrect to suggest that accounting practices that adhere to applicable law are somehow askew.

NNSA agrees efforts to produce information which better supports decision making from existing data can be improved; however, we believe that the report does not currently clarify and balance discussion regarding the contractors' accounting practices. We therefore request that the GAO clearly state that NNSA accounting practices adhere to public law applicable to all government contractors. It should also be pointed out that the Department has an unqualified external audit opinion, supporting the fair and accurate presentation of its accounting data.

3

Response to GAO Draft Report, GAO-13-534
"NATIONAL NUCLEAR SECURITY ADMINSTRATION: Laboratories' Indirect Cost
Management Has Improved but Additional Opportunities Exist"

<u>Technical Comments</u>

1. Page 13, 3rd bullet titled "Distribution" - The last sentence of this bullet states "Because of these differences, indirect costs were spread across different program costs at Lawrence Livermore.' This statement is misleading. The use of a Value Added Base (VAB) does not result in indirect costs being spread over fewer program costs. With the use of a VAB, fully burdened labor costs appear to be higher than fully burdened material costs. Overall, the programs receive their proportional share of the General and Administrative (G&A) costs.

2. Page 18, 1st bullet – This bullet currently states:

    •   In March 2009, OFFM and NNSA site officials determined that the M&O contractor's indirect cost allocation model for Lawrence Livermore did not fully comply with Cost Accounting Standards. Specifically, the model did not require some programs, such as science and technology strategic planning and laboratory outreach programs, to contribute the standard cost allocation amounts for General and Administrative indirect costs at the laboratory. According to NNSA officials, the M&O contractor allowed this practice to occur because it believed that these programs did not equitably benefit from the activities covered by these indirect costs. OFFM officials disagreed, and the M&O contractor changed its cost allocation model in fiscal year 2013 to more equitably share these indirect costs across all programs.

    For clarity and accuracy, please restate the bullet as follows:

    •   "In March 2009, OFFM and NNSA site officials determined that the M&O contractor's indirect cost allocation model for Lawrence Livermore did not fully comply with Cost Accounting Standards. Specifically, activities such as science and technology strategic planning and laboratory outreach were included in the Strategic Mission Support (SMS) pool. These costs were viewed by LLNL as broadly institutional in the same manner as G&A. According to NNSA officials, the M&O contractor allowed this practice to occur because it believed that these programs would be better monitored if they remained separate from G&A. OFFM officials disagreed, and the M&O contractor changed its cost allocation model in fiscal year 2013 to include these indirect costs in the G&A pool."

4

Appendix IV: GAO Contact and Staff Acknowledgments

GAO Contact	David C. Trimble, (202) 512-3841 or trimbled@gao.gov
Staff Acknowledgments	In addition to the contact named above, Janet Frisch, Assistant Director; Paul Kinney; Mehrzad Nadji; Alison O'Neill; Christopher Pacheco; Sophia Payind; Cheryl Peterson; Steven Putansu; Kiki Theodoropoulos; Nick Weeks; and William Woods made key contributions to this report.

GAO's Mission	The Government Accountability Office, the audit, evaluation, and investigative arm of Congress, exists to support Congress in meeting its constitutional responsibilities and to help improve the performance and accountability of the federal government for the American people. GAO examines the use of public funds; evaluates federal programs and policies; and provides analyses, recommendations, and other assistance to help Congress make informed oversight, policy, and funding decisions. GAO's commitment to good government is reflected in its core values of accountability, integrity, and reliability.
Obtaining Copies of GAO Reports and Testimony	The fastest and easiest way to obtain copies of GAO documents at no cost is through GAO's website (http://www.gao.gov). Each weekday afternoon, GAO posts on its website newly released reports, testimony, and correspondence. To have GAO e-mail you a list of newly posted products, go to http://www.gao.gov and select "E-mail Updates."
Order by Phone	The price of each GAO publication reflects GAO's actual cost of production and distribution and depends on the number of pages in the publication and whether the publication is printed in color or black and white. Pricing and ordering information is posted on GAO's website, http://www.gao.gov/ordering.htm.
	Place orders by calling (202) 512-6000, toll free (866) 801-7077, or TDD (202) 512-2537.
	Orders may be paid for using American Express, Discover Card, MasterCard, Visa, check, or money order. Call for additional information.
Connect with GAO	Connect with GAO on Facebook, Flickr, Twitter, and YouTube. Subscribe to our RSS Feeds or E-mail Updates. Listen to our Podcasts. Visit GAO on the web at www.gao.gov.
To Report Fraud, Waste, and Abuse in Federal Programs	Contact:
	Website: http://www.gao.gov/fraudnet/fraudnet.htm E-mail: fraudnet@gao.gov Automated answering system: (800) 424-5454 or (202) 512-7470
Congressional Relations	Katherine Siggerud, Managing Director, siggerudk@gao.gov, (202) 512-4400, U.S. Government Accountability Office, 441 G Street NW, Room 7125, Washington, DC 20548
Public Affairs	Chuck Young, Managing Director, youngc1@gao.gov, (202) 512-4800 U.S. Government Accountability Office, 441 G Street NW, Room 7149 Washington, DC 20548

Please Print on Recycled Paper.